MRS BEETON'S CHRISTMAS PLUM PUDDING

(Average cost 3 Shillings and 6d)

Text: CHARLOTTE CORY

rai - sins, A pound__ and a half of bread-crumbs mix; Then

rai - sins, A pound__ and a half of bread-crumbs mix, do mix; Then

rai - sins, A pound__ and a half of bread-crumbs mix, do mix; Then

rai - sins, A pound__ and a half of bread-crumbs mix; Then

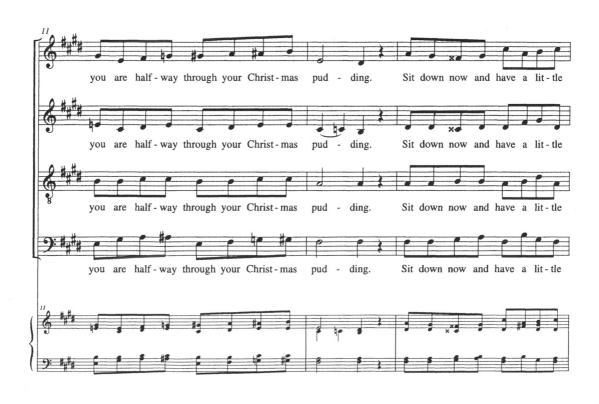

you are half-way through your Christ-mas pud - ding. Sit down now and have a lit-tle

you are half-way through your Christ-mas pud - ding. Sit down now and have a lit-tle

you are half-way through your Christ-mas pud - ding. Sit down now and have a lit-tle

you are half-way through your Christ-mas pud - ding. Sit down now and have a lit-tle

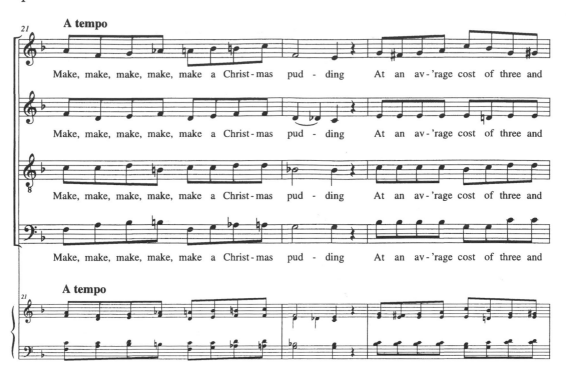

mix; Eight well-bea-ten eggs, a pound of su - gar, A

mix, do mix; Eight well-bea-ten eggs, a pound of su - gar, A

mix, do mix; Eight well-bea-ten eggs, a pound of su - gar, A

mix; Eight well-bea-ten eggs, a pound of su - gar, A

wine-glass full of ve-ree best bran-dee. Make sure your Christ-mas pud-ding is well

wine-glass full of ve-ree best bran-dee, best bran-dee. Make sure your Christ-mas pud-ding is well

wine-glass full of ve-ree best bran-dee, best bran-dee. Make sure your Christ-mas pud-ding is well

wine-glass full of ve-ree best bran-dee, best bran-dee. Make sure your Christ-mas pud-ding is well

blen - ded And your fam - 'ly hap - py ev - er more shall be.

blen - ded And your fam - 'ly hap - py ev - er more shall be, hap - py shall

blen - ded And your fam - 'ly hap - py ev - er more shall be, hap - py shall

blen - ded And your fam - 'ly hap - py ev - er more shall be.

Meno mosso ♩ = 104

(Finger clicks)

(Finger clicks)

be.

(Finger clicks)

be.

Soli *loose, swung*

(Finger clicks)

_ Ba da ba da ba doo dah,_ ba da ba da ba doo dah, ba da ba da ba doo dah,.

Tutti finger clicks

Meno mosso ♩ = 104

Now Ma - dam, tie it tight - ly__ and boil, boil, boil but on - ly light - ly.__

Now Ma - dam, tie it tight - ly__ and boil, boil, boil but on - ly light - ly.__

yeah! Now Ma - dam, tie it tight - ly__ and boil, boil, boil but on - ly light - ly.__

yeah! Now Ma - dam, tie it tight - ly__ and boil, boil, boil but on - ly light - ly.__

Telephone ring*
(old fashioned)

Hum__

Hum__

Hum__

Hum__ oh

Male voice** "To purchase moulds in every shape and size, make to visit for this enterprise, Messrs R & J Slack, who are located –
(spoken in a posh, BBC voice 'like Lord Reith')

*optional
**with megaphone (optional)

*with megaphone (optional)

10

*optional

12

On Christ-mas Day,— first thing in the morn - ing, Fetch your pud-ding wait-ing in the

On Christ-mas Day,— first thing in the morn - ing, Fetch your pud-ding wait-ing in the

On Christ-mas Day,— first thing in the morn - ing, Fetch your pud-ding wait-ing in the

On Christ-mas Day,— first thing in the morn - ing, Fetch your pud-ding wait-ing in the

store.   Plunge in - to a vat of boil - ing wa - ter:

store.   Plunge in - to a vat of boil - ing wa - ter:

store.   Plunge in -. to a vat of boil - ing wa - ter:

store.   Plunge in - to a vat of boil - ing wa - ter:

Boil at least an-oth-er hour or more. When the pud-ding sure is steam-ing

Boil at least an-oth-er hour or more._____ When the pud-ding sure is steam-ing

Boil at least an-oth-er hour or more._____ When the pud-ding sure is steam-ing

Boil at least an-oth-er hour or more. When the pud-ding sure is steam-ing

Female
Oh at least!

nice - ly, Turn it firm-ly out on-to a plate.

nice - ly, Turn it firm-ly out on-to a plate._____

nice - ly, Turn it firm-ly out on-to a plate.__

nice - ly, Turn it firm-ly out on-to a plate._____

Both
Fire - proof plate!

Plant a sprig of hol-ly in the mid - dle, It can-not grow but it will de - co-

Plant a sprig of hol-ly in the mid - dle, It can-not grow but it will de - co-

Plant a sprig of hol-ly in the mid - dle, It can-not grow but it will de - co-

Plant a sprig of hol-ly in the mid - dle, It can-not grow but it will de - co-

- rate._____ Fill a wine glass full of fine French

- rate, will de - co - rate. Fill a wine glass full of fine French

- rate, will de - co - rate. Fill a wine glass full of fine French

- rate._____ Fill a wine glass full of fine French

Both

One more time!

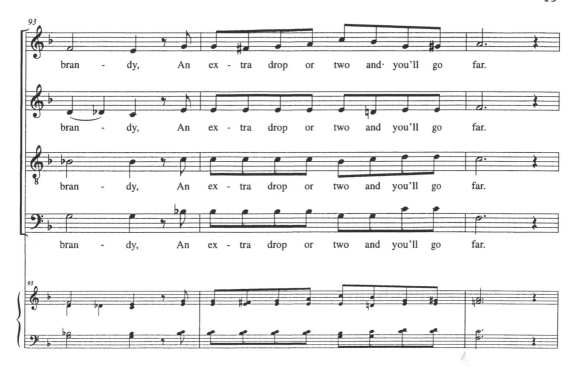

bran - dy, An ex - tra drop or two and you'll go far.

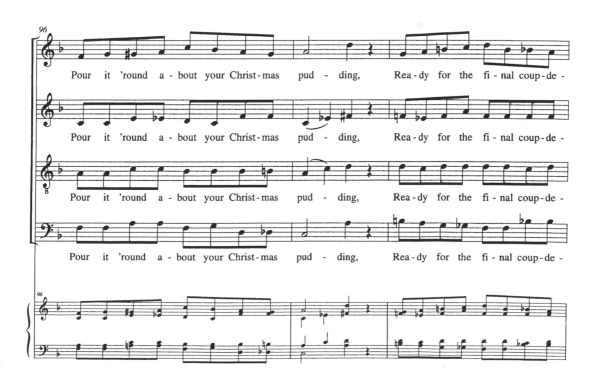

Pour it 'round a - bout your Christ - mas pud - ding, Rea - dy for the fi - nal coup - de -

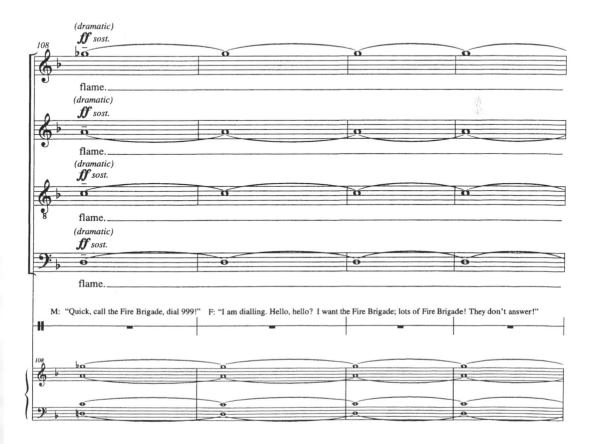

Printed in England 10/11 (179914)